I0106546

A Fathering Spirit

K. Lee

KLC Publishing

A Fathering Spirit

K. Lee

Published by Krystal Lee Enterprises (KLE Publishing) Please send comments and questions:
Krystal Lee Enterprises
770-240-0089 Ext. 1
sales@KLEPub.com
To Reach the Author:
Email: me@drkrystallee.com me@authorklee.com
Web: AuthorKLee.com
Social Media All Channels: @AuthorKLee

Printed in the United States of America.

ISBN: 978-1-945066-79-5

Thank you to every father who has a heart for children.

Thank you to my Lord and Savior Yashua, Jesus the Christ. Special thanks to my children, family, and friends.

To you the reader, may you be encouraged and uplifted from reading this book.

Shalom,

K. Lee

A Fathering Spirit

K. Lee

Table of Contents

Chapter Prelude

Becoming a father is a day that lodges in the minds of expecting fathers. The day, the time, and what they planned to do with their lives sometimes shifts in that moment when you realize your life is no longer about you, but the baby before you. You make room to include this baby in your plans, and you determine that you must become a provider.

For some of us, we see the example when we are young and we pray that some day we, too, will become a father. In the lion kingdom, a male lion has to be intentional for becoming a father. He has to prove his ability to lead and manage a home, his dominion. There is stiff competition, and his role is not to be made light of.

The role of a father, like a lion, is to protect the wife and the children. He is to keep a watchful eye on what is happening around his dominion so he knows how to protect his home. The partnerships he makes with other male lions are a joint work. They each have to hold their own, but together, they realize they can cover more ground.

Lions do not fight together, but they take down their own prey and bring their works home to their family. They keep large predators away and equip the family to survive while he is away. He trails behind a pregnant wife to ensure the safety of the new cub. He is present, even if he watches from a distance. A father is watchful and is not afraid to stand up for his family, no matter the odds against him.

He has the ability to chill and relax, and only takes off to chase a worthy prey. He is calculated and considers what his desired outcome is. A father, like a lion, has a plan for his house, although he faces the unknown.

This incredible creature, the lion, proves that we have the instinct to rise to the occasion to protect our women and children. When we band together, we can learn from each other and teach the young lions, men, how to love, provide, and take care of their homes as well. When they are learning, they should remain with older lions that can teach them what they don't know.

Young lions, men, should build bonds with other men who are heading in their direction and want out of life what they also seek. How can two walk together if they don't agree (Amos 3:3)? If you seek to walk in a father role, become a father, or be a better father, the life of a lion lays a foundation. How can you achieve what you don't know? How can you improve what you don't know is broken?

I want to let you know that this book is not about what you have to do, or even what you hope to have tomorrow, but how you can work with today to build the tomorrow Yah has in mind for you. Allow me to further explain.

Chapter 1
Introduction

In Genesis, the Father of Creation created Adam. In making him, He made him complete, having all he needed for life within him. He was assigned to name the animals and live amongst them.

In the Garden, Adam lived in the presence of Yah and was connected to His image, the heavens, and the Word. They were in community living in peace. The Father of Creation could walk amongst Adam in the cool of the day!

But Adam desired companionship to even create like His master designer. The Father, knowing the heart of His son, made him with the intention to multiply and continue his dominion on earth. The Creator made him a father because He gave life to Eve. Father God took a rib from him and made a man with a womb, and Adam called her womb-man or woman.

The ceremony to transition a daughter from her

father to her husband, in essence, is an exchange of responsibility from one to the other. A husband covers his wife. I heard it once explained to me by a wise man that your husband becomes the father of the bride–in that he takes on all the responsibility of a father for her life.

How incredible to know that before there was a mother, we had a father who was willing to father the nations! No, he was not perfect. Yes, Adam made mistakes at being a father to his wife and to his children. Yes, fathers today are guilty of the same thing because we are not God, although we are made in His likeness (Genesis 1:27). But the good news here is that they chose, like Adam, to be fathers.

Yahweh chose to father Christ, and bring His Son to earth so that He can redeem many—all who believe in Him and accept the gift of salvation (Galatians 3:13). We may not have the best or ideal situation with our fathers, but their purpose for life is important. We can learn from our creation story and the experiences of fathers in the Bible.

This is not to say there is no value in a mother; she has a purpose too, and ultimately, they are to work together, men and women, to raise families and build communities. This book is not to discredit the marvelous work in women, but to express the intention for how men, fathers, and those willing to father can see how God provides and instructs how to father.

For those who never had a father or didn't have a healthy relationship with their own father, this book will bring comfort and direction. This book is a celebration of fatherhood and the assignment put on men's shoulders to lead by example. You are the first field of defense for the home, and you too need a strong foundation. That foundation, I would argue, needs to be rooted in God, Yahweh.

In this book, I present twelve fathers of note from the Bible. Adam was the first father to humanity, and it could be tempting to blame the failures of humanity on him, but we all should bear the weight. In life, no one person is responsible for all of anyone's problems.

Furthermore, no one person should be such a great influence on your life except Yahweh, God, the Holy Father. To understand the plight against humanity, we need to revisit how we all fall short of the glory of God, perfection. In each of our stories, we will journey through the imperfections and the knowledge we choose to do wrong instead of right. Not every example will be your story, and if some of the examples are your story, good news, God has a response for that!

Although Yahweh is perfect, He has love and compassion for us. Be encouraged by this book, and allow the lesson and blessing of each story to bring comfort and direction for you to live in love.

Chapter 2
Yahweh

To know a true father, we have to consider the character of Yah, God Almighty. This book can never be big enough to tell it all, so I will pull out a few key points that I believe will help fathers and their children. In this case, we can only present a good father example.

So, a good father makes provision. Before the Father put Adam on earth, He prepared a place for him. He gave him a house, a purpose, and a role for humanity. He considered his wants but also supplied his needs.

It was God who said, "It is not good that man be alone" (Genesis 2:18). He created us for connection. He provided Eve and gave Adam a choice. A father knows the way, but he coaches his children to learn it. He gives them the confidence to decide.

Adam chose Eve, and God held him responsible for

his choice to make her his wife. A good father supports the choices and convictions of his children. He sets the foundation for what is good, but he lets them decide with consequences.

When Adam messed up, there was a penalty. A good father must judge and correct poor behavior. Although Yah is Lord and judge, He is also redeemer. In the Father and Son relationship between Yahweh and Yashua, God and Jesus, you can see more of the heart of God. He is the same from all times without a beginning or end. He said He would send a Savior to be a lamb to carry away the sins of men (people).

His Son, He used to make provision for His creation. We don't live off bread alone, but every word from the Son (Matthew 4:4). So a good father cares for his legacy and his children's children. He will do a great work when people see it and are grateful, but also when they don't.

The Savior was born and did great works for people who still wouldn't accept his gift of salvation. Today, many can witness a miracle performed in Jesus' name and still choose not to believe in His power but want His blessing. The goodness about God is that while we were still sinners, He died to be a ransom for many (Romans 5:8-9). As a father, God gave so that anyone who believes in Him could have a Good Father and everlasting life!

A father will make a way out of no way. A good father, like a good shepherd, takes the problems of his flock and prays for direction. They teach to bless what they have and to be grateful because that opens doors for miracles. The Messiah took bread and a fish, prayed, blessed it, and lifted it to heaven. Then, the Holy Father provided a miracle.

He gave more than they needed and instructed them not to waste. The Father will give you all that you need and more. How you see it shapes your response. Your heart posture does control if you will witness a miracle or tick another box of disappointment.

Yashua fed the people out of the blessing, and he expects us to do the same. As we receive from our Heavenly Father, we are to be grateful and give, trusting in God to provide. God says obedience is greater than sacrifice (1 Samuel 15:22). He teaches the importance of doing the will of God instead of leaning on your own understanding. If you need a good father, you want to start by looking at the Holy Father, who I pray is your father.

He teaches us to love not because it's earned, but because He first loved us (1 John 4:19). We do it to be a reflection of His teachings and to show our gratitude for His goodness.

About Yahweh

Having an example of a good father is extremely healthy. Yahweh brought His Son to earth to be an example to humanity. He demonstrates through His consistent character of fathering Adam to Christ, the expectations he has for the role of a father. They are to provide, to instruct, and to discipline.

Assignment: Study the foundation of a good father again and consider what you are doing right or could improve upon.

Your Impact: Mentoring. Those who have been gifted to be a father with structure, provision, and direction, consider speaking into the lives of other young men and women who could use your gift and time.

Make it Personal

Reflection

Point 1: Yah gave Adam a place to live and provided what he needed.

Point 2: He also cared for what he wanted and made provision for that.

Point 3: There is a consequence for not following the rules, and that discipline has to be there for the household.

Point 4: Christ is a living example of mercy, patience, and being long-suffering for your children.

Point 5: Although Yah could have given up on humanity after Adam, He continued to teach and father him through his life changes.

Affirmation

I am not perfect, but I am loved, and God gave me an assignment to be a provider and correct wrong behaviour.

Chapter 3
Eli

Yahweh was clear on a standard for humanity. He outlined the expectations in the Ten Commandments and further explained them in the books of Leviticus, Deuteronomy, and Exodus. There are a lot of rules, and the New Testament sums them up with love your neighbor as yourself, and love God with all your heart and essence (Galatians 5:14). We are to be obedient out of love and follow the commandments of Yah to demonstrate that love for Him.

Our God is a God of action, and not mere lip service. Some of us are faithful to God, but we may not know how to apply that love we have for God to our families. It can be tempting to go along to get along and keep our convictions quiet when they should be evident in our actions and response to anyone.

Can it be possible to be a good man of Yah and a terrible father? To know the Word, but fall short of implementing the Word to the point of even turning a blind eye to sin? Knowing the example of a good father in part is enough to see how any father will fail to even compare to Yahweh.

The structure that Yah gives in how He fathers creation and relates to His Son should make the world want to take note. Yet, many read the Word and fail to implement what they learn, or even try. Eli, for example, was a mighty man of God who failed to implement the things of God with his children.

He ran the temple, the church, when it was so holy that only a select few could enter. The holies of holies, some would die because they were not holy, and there would be a bell on their feet to alert the staff outside the tent, to drag their bodies out because they died within the presence of God. For Eli to stand here and survive, you would think all of his life must have been perfect.

People came to Eli to ask for him to pray and seek God on their behalf. He would advise the people, the church, and children for how to serve God and honor Him. Yet, he turned a muted ear toward the Father's Word concerning his children.

Eli knew how to be loyal to the Word of God for everyone else and to do the work required by God. He was obedient, but he began to sacrifice for the sins of his sons instead of bringing correction. He knew about their sins, and although he didn't condone them, he turned a blind eye by not correcting them.

Fathers can be tempted to have an excuse for why they exit and escape discipline. Many fathers are tempted to leave this task to the mother so that she can drop the hammer on discipline. Yet, this is not her job. God expects you, fathers and those with a fathering spirit, to show up for children. There is an authority a father has to seed deep into the hearts of children; don't mute your voice.

Have you noticed the response to an active father in the household? Everyone is attentive, even if they don't agree. They will hold their tongue when they know how to reverence their father's position. Respect is greatly taught by the father in the home. Respect is what the Bible says men need, and likewise, they must share, earn, and teach (Ephesians 5:33).

How can you expect to have something you don't teach or exemplify? The issue Eli had with his boys is that he did not teach respect for God or himself to his sons. The mother isn't mentioned, so could it be that she wasn't held responsible for the father's job? Eli was told to correct and enforce correction with his sons.

It is not enough to speak up; there has to be a consequence or a recourse for bad behavior to work correction. Yah had a consequence to disobedience, and we should too. Mercy is fine, it's in the role, but learn behavior and true repentance is required.

Because Eli failed to father in this way, his sacrifice to go along to get along cost him a legacy. His children were both killed on the same day. His grandchildren were cursed to not own anything, to beg, and to die before the age of 25! Wow, can fathers or their families afford for them not to discipline even if others don't like it?

Can anyone afford not to father their children and teach accountability? Eli's sons slept with women in the church, ate food that was for God, stole, and committed other vile acts that cost their lives and changed the future for their children.

About Eli

Eli was a mighty man of God, and he was faithful to serve in the temple. He was appreciated by the congregation, but he was not respected by his sons. He failed to raise his sons to reverence Yah and the church. When he discovered the terrible behavior of his sons, he did not correct or enforce any consequences. By not correcting his sons, God had to correct them. Eli reminds each of us of the importance of reprimanding our children.

Assignment: Correct the bad behavior in your home now, so you don't have to deal with the judgment of God for what you did not correct.

Your Impact: Discipline. Discipline is not a punishment, but an act of love. When you change how you see discipline, it will give you the eyes to see how it saves.

Make it Personal

Reflection

Point 1: Eli was a great man of God, faithful to serve.

Point 2: He was not a good father, although he could have been if he had corrected his sons.

Point 3: By not correcting his sons, he obligated Yah to correct and humble them.

Point 4: His sons were killed, and his legacy was limited.

Point 5: Teach your children the way and enforce correction to expand your legacy.

Affirmation

I will not be more concerned about how people feel about me than honoring God in how I correct bad behavior.

Chapter 4
Job

Teaching boundaries and expectations brings rewards. Working hard and teaching your children to honor that will also bring benefits. One of the easiest to recognize benefits is that you create a connection within your family. You create structure for your house and business, too.

Job was also a mighty man of Yah. He was faithful to his wife and good to his children. He was such a man and example that even God bragged about him (Job 1:8). Down on earth, Job loved a wife who benefited from his diligence. He was faithful in building on what he had started with. He had land and servants to keep his grounds.

He was a businessman and a farmer who knew how to keep animals and till the ground. His family grew, and he had many children. His children were blessed to have a strong foundation, financial security, and to be loved by both parents. To make things better, all his children were good-looking and well-mannered.

Job and his wife raised their children with structure and expectations. Job's children mirrored his example, and so they all loved God. He spent time with his children and told them the value of spending time with one another. Because of their close connection, they were all close, and on a regular basis, they sat and ate together.

The Bible says in Job that his children would gather monthly to read the Bible, pray, and eat dinner together (Job 1:13-19). They had a frequent family reunion, and God was at the center of the family. Even the devil said–and I paraphrase, "Job worships you because you have a hedge of protection around him. If you take it away, he won't serve you." The Father can permit the enemy to touch you to prove a point about your character. We are all tempted, but we are not tempted by Yah, but we can be tested by Him.

The Father wanted to prove something about His servant Job, and the book proves that we are his servants and not the other way around. In this test, Job loss everything. He loss his servants, his animals, and all his children when they were in a Bible study and died. He loss everything in a few days, and even his wife turned his life sour. She told him in Job 2:19, "Do you still hold fast your integrity? Curse God and die."

Have bad things befell your life, your children, or your business? Have things gone from good to terrible, and you don't know why? I know it can be hard to serve God when you feel like He hates you because your children die young, or people die at times you think are premature. We can grow bitter like Job's Wife and believe we should just die and give up. Job wanted to give up and even cursed his mother's breasts for nursing him to life.

When we are hurting, it is hard to be full of faith and see the future beyond the trees. When you raised your children to stay out of trouble, come in before dark, don't do this or that, and a stray bullet hits them or a drunk driver takes their life. It can be hard to mourn the life of your children when you know that they should outlive you, and so should your grandchildren.

He was mourning, and so was his wife. Job was a faithful father, and he was good to his servants and all he had. It can be hard to lose it all when you haven't done anything to deserve it. I want to encourage you not to blame yourself or allow others to pin blame on you. Remember Job's friends who said it was his fault for his suffering. They accused him by saying something like, "Surely you did something to deserve this. Why would God let this happen unless you are a thief or did something wrong that we don't know?"

Job professed his innocence to no avail. Some fathers get blamed for why their children are dead. I am sure his wife blamed him or even God for not keeping their children. Having a child born dead or dying at birth can equally be hard. But Job stayed with a wife who blamed God and was bitter towards him. He was reminded that he is a vessel in the Hand of God, called for His purpose and not his own.

When he lost everything and was stricken in his body with boils, living in constant pain, he felt like dying as he endured his misery. He found strength in the words from the Father to pull him up. In times like these, we need to be around iron that can sharpen the iron within you. People who can be strong when you are weak.

The wife who told him to die was a part of a blessing the Father poured out on his household. He got more children, more servants, and was restored to more than he had before. His faithfulness blessed his family. If he had allowed pain to overshadow the power of God, he could have lost all hope and not seen anything beyond death and heartbreak. Job, staying in the fire at the Father's behest, he received a double portion and exemplified a father with a heart reaching for the standards of God.

About Job

Job was a faithful steward over what he had. He had a family, a business, and a farm, all of which he took care of. He could be trusted, and even the Father called him "upright." The devil said that Job wouldn't be faithful if he took it all away, and the Father permitted his testing. He lost his children, his wife became bitter, and he lost his cattle and wealth seemingly overnight. Even in the midst of all this, he did not stop believing but stayed with his family and, most importantly, with Yah. He had to deal with the loss of his children and the bitterness of his wife. He didn't run away from the pain but allowed God to heal him and his wife.

Assignment: If you have been beating yourself up, and you have done all you can, and bad news hits, pray that the love of God fills your heart.

Your Impact: Love. Allow the love of God to heal your heart and help you to forgive and live. Don't abandon those who are here to love you.

Make it Personal

Reflection

Point 1: Job was doing everything right.

Point 2: Even though we do everything right, bad things, or testing, can still come our way.

Point 3: When his wife told him to disown God and die, he knew that was her broken heart speaking, and he did not judge her in the moment. He stayed with her.

Point 4: Allowing Yah to heal his heart, he opened his marriage and life to the restoration of God.

Point 5: The Father is faithful to help us recover it all, and in the case of Job, he got more children, and his wife was able to love again.

Affirmation

Even through my test, I will not disown Father God, but choose to love hin and my family through difficult times.

Chapter 5
Isaac

Isaac was the son of Abraham and Sarah, the son of the promise. He was born to parents who desired to have him, and so he entered the world with love. Children who are hoped for, when they come, are celebrated when they arrive, and even spoiled.

Isaac was married to Rebekah, a woman chosen for him and spotted by her willingness to fetch water (Genesis 24). The two of them had a pair of twins, Esau and Jacob. These twins represented two nations that started their battle in the womb. Esau was born first, with Jacob holding on to his heel (Genesis 25:26). This was and still is a serious sibling rivalry unresolved.

Esau was the chosen favorite of his father, and Jacob the chosen of their mother. The family was divided by favoritism. The dad chose Esau because he was strong, fierce, and had manly features about his character and presence.

Perhaps, he reminded him of himself or how he wanted to be seen? He was a man's man, whereas Jacob was not.

Jacob was not the child who appeared to receive the approval of his dad. He may have been too skinny, not bold enough, or otherwise struggled to gain the attention of his father. Based on his birth order, he would have been destined to inherit nothing and work under his brother's hand for everything he had unless he became a self-made man.

He had no birthright and would likely not receive a blessing either. Yet, the Father in heaven had a plan for Jacob that he and his mother did not want to leave to chance. There was a promise spoken over Jacob's life, but he and Rebekah thought they had to conspire and cheat to get it. They couldn't see him rising above Esau by looking at his drawbacks, his size, inability to hunt, or the challenge to win the affection of his father to get the birthright or blessing honorably.

How many of you know that, just as Father had a plan for Jacob's life, he knows the plan he has for your life and your children. Even when our natural father doesn't know who we are or what we will become, our Heavenly Father does know our purpose (Jeremiah 29:11). We can have confidence in knowing He will make a way for His promises to be established in the earth–nothing He says to come forth will be denied (Isaiah 55:11).

Although Rebekah knew Jacob was great and God was too, she was willing to follow the example of Isaac and choose her favorite son over the plans of God. She got Jacob to dress up and look like Esau and bring his father, Isaac, food. After eating the wonderfully prepared game, he blessed Jacob.

The truth was, Jacob was already blessed because his Heavenly Father spoke it over his life. It is nice to get a blessing from his father, but even if his dad didn't do it, God did it already. Over the years, Esau fought to get the blessing and to return the birthright he sold for a bowl of beans to Jacob. A fool and wealth will soon depart (Proverbs 21:20). Jacob, for tricking his father, was judged and suffered a consequence.

Esau was also judged for selling his birthright. Both sons had no respect for their parent, who didn't favor them, and this division caused a sibling rivalry that has never ended. To this day, Jacob, who became Israel, fights with Esau over the birthright. If Isaac vowed to squash the separation and bridge the gap between his sons, maybe there could be peace? As a father, you are to establish order and respect within your home. When you fail to do that, the whole house will follow suit.

About Isaac

Isaac was a father who had a pair of twins, Esau, the oldest, and Jacob. He loved his sons, but he related better to one than another. The son he related to the most, he spent the most time with, and prepared to leave everything he had with, based on birthright cultural standards and his desire. He did show favoritism toward his son Esau and Rebekah to Jacob. Jacob was a trickster and cheated his father. The rivalry between the siblings could have been squashed early on if Isaac had order in his home instead of dualing pairs.

Assignment: Try to find a connection with children who might be hard for you to understand because they are less like you.

Your Impact: Understanding. Doing something that you don't typically do to better understand your children can build a bridge of compassion that can extend to you.

Make it Personal

Reflection

Point 1: Isaac ignored the issue between the brothers and connected with the son most like him.

Point 2: Esau was the son who was the man's man and, based on birth order, should have gotten it all.

Point 3: Rebekah heard a prophecy that she did not know how it would come about and thought to intervene by conspiring with Jacob to swindle Esau and Isaac.

Point 4: The decisions of the sons did not go unpunished, and the Father in heaven judged them both.

Point 5: If there are issues between children, it is best to address the problems so that they don't escalate and grow worse over the years to come.

Affirmation

If there are issues between my children, or even if I don't feel like I can relate fully with my son or daughter, I will not show favoritism to cause division, but make differences a rooted strength for my family.

Chapter 6
Noah

Noah, a man whom we all know was not perfect. He was a man with a habitual drinking problem that was written about in the scriptures. He was called at a dark time when the world seemed to have given way to the cultural demands to blend faith, genes, and other unclean acts. The Father says that Noah was the only one pure and his family (Genesis 6:9).

Not sure the depths of that statement because it can be argued that gene splicing, joining animal DNA with human DNA, and other acts were happening even back in these times–and the Father hated it. He did not like humans partaking with angels or mixing blood with creatures. He wanted to start life anew and rid the earth of what he detested.

He gave Noah the assignment to gather every beast, small and great, and put them on the ark. Only, he had to build the ark first with very specific instructions. He had to find the wood, and it is not clear if he did most of this work himself with some help or alone. Many thought he was crazy to build a boat on dry land. He would try to warn people about what was to come, but no one would heed his warning.

Have you ever tried to tell people a storm was coming, and no one lifted a finger to prepare? They didn't get water, have a flashlight, batteries, nothing. They just assumed God would provide when they could have prevented the fallout that would ensue. Noah was a good father who cared for his children and grandchildren.

He also cared for nature and all the animals the Lord cared about. He put them on the boat, plus the provision of food for the journey, and remained on the boat for forty days and nights. He had to listen to sibling quarrels, women getting sick, and I can imagine animals trying to get out of hand. Can you imagine trying to break up a fight between two gorillas? Or dealing with birds flying all around because they want out?

It could have been stressful on that boat. Staying sober-minded is a requirement of God, but He also inspired the text, "Drink and be merry" (Ecclesiastes 8:15). I am sure there were days he said, "I need a drink, Father." Moments when cuss words were said, and he lost his temper. There may be days you say that, too, or you lose it and have a cussing session to get it all out. I am not condoning drunkenness or cussing, and neither does the Bible or the Word of God, but He understands.

If you are dealing with an addiction or a problem that you want to end and are struggling, the Father can still use you mightily to father your children and a nation. Three nations came from Noah. He was born on a continent that didn't even like albinos and would kill them–yet he survived. You might be battling something or everything, but you can be a great father despite your personal challenges. Noah proves that we can please God even if we may look like a failure to people.

About Noah

Noah wasn't a perfect man or father, but he was a good father who sought to protect his children. Noah was a faithful servant of Yah, who also liked to drink. He drank a lot, to the point sometimes to where he would blackout. Although he could have been misunderstood by people, the Father gave him the assignment to save not only his family but also all the animals in his proximity. He built the ark to hold himself, his sons, their wives, and his wife. He did the command of God concerning his family when everyone thought he was crazy and found favor for all nations.

Assignment: If you are doing the great work of fathering your children, continue to do that because your faithfulness will bless all of your children.

Your Impact: Favor. If you want the favor of God on the lives of your children, do the will of Yah, and He will bless your children and all those in your house.

Make it Personal

Reflection

Point 1: Noah was a faithful follower of Yahweh.

Point 2: He provided for his family by building the ark to protect them during the 40-day and 40-night flood.

Point 3: He was willing to work when no one else was around, or commended his actions.

Point 4: He kept order on the boat and was faithful to save the animals alive.

Point 5: Each of his sons received an inheritance of land, people, and a nation. When you do right by the Father, He will find a way to bless everyone in your home, no matter their birth order.

Affirmation

I will be faithful to honor God even if I am flawed, and strive to be a good father to bring favor on my children.

Chapter 7
Jacob/Israel

Jacob, a product of a house divided, didn't learn from the mistakes of his parents. When we are born into dysfunction or raised to value an understanding, it is hard to break that mold. It is far more natural to fall into the familiar and repeat old history. Familiar spirits love to entrap families and their legacies by sending the same demons or spirits to plague a family because it worked on the father or mother.

We must learn from our parents what worked and what was a challenge, then prepare our children to overcome what we failed at. What we learn, we want to share with them, so they don't repeat our mistakes.

Jacob was in a family that prized the grave sin of favoritism. He tried to show equal love to his sons, and he did until Joseph, the son of love, was born. Jacob falls in love with Rachel and agrees to work for seven years to marry her. He was tricked, however, into marrying her twin sister, born with a lazy eye, Leah. He didn't know who he had in his bedchamber until the next day when he saw her, and I am sure he got the shock of his life.

Like how he tricked his father, he too was tricked in the dark. How you treat your parents does matter, and the Bible says to honor your father and mother so that your days will be long (Exodus 20:12). We don't pick our parents or their flaws. We are to love them with their flaws and trust the Father to repay what man cannot. We can choose who we allow to father us, however.

Jacob fled home after taking all that he could from Esau, and he dreaded the day he would return because of what he had done to his father and Esau. But he would have to come home and face the music. We cannot run away from our troubles, but will someday have to face them, prayerfully, before our parents go into the grave.

Now, Jacob had to work seven more years to marry Rachel, and he did. The woman he loved could not bear children, so she had her maidservant bear children on her behalf. Leah had many children, and she also gave her maidservant to bear children. There were twelve sons born between four women, and to all of the children, he was the father.

He had to deal with four women, all with demands of some kind or complaints. His sons were used to working together because they lived on a farm and had to provide for this large family. Their sisters are not included in the twelve count of sons. After amassing much wealth, he was told to go home after being cheated twice by his father-in-law.

His lying and cheating ways caught up with him

for how he treated his parents. Then comes how he treated his own children when Joseph was born. Joseph was a son he prayed would have come years earlier. He was younger than his brothers and was the child, I think, who looked the most like Rachel. He was handsome and, most importantly, reminded him of Rachel.

His wife died giving birth to Benjamin, and the other ladies helped to raise them. I am sure, though, it was grief and torment to see his wife in his son. His heart was to show his love for a wife long gone, with the son who remained. I don't think he made Joseph a favorite just because he was born of a woman he loved–I think it was the largest reason, but I also think it was because he was grieving her death and he didn't know how to get unstuck or to show the love he had for her with others.

Sometimes fathers can get stuck, and the love they have can't be released because they are torn on the inside. Maybe he also saw the favor of God on his life, and he honored that, but the sons could not see that either. He made the coat of many colors for Joseph himself. Can you imagine a man sewing or weaving a garment? What would make a man do that? A farmer at that? Love.

When the brothers thought to take their revenge out on Joseph and kill him out of jealousy, they assumed they would be loved more. It did not work, though. He was bedridden instead, and he didn't move much for years in the absence of his reminder of Rachel. Now she was truly gone, and the sons saw how much grief it caused for Joseph to be gone–not even Benjamin could curb his grief.

That also helps to conclude that maybe it wasn't just about children from Rachel, but how Joseph favored her so much. He missed Rachel and Joseph. If your father is stuck on his first love, or he may spend more time with a child over others, try not to get vengeful. Try to be compassionate and give them the space they may need to overcome their grief. Give situations like this to God, and try to love the brother/sister you have, because a father's choice should not be a slight against other children.

I didn't grow up with my father, but my half-brothers did. They knew him in ways I never would, and although we are all adults with children of our own, he still has a different connection with each of us that we had to grow to accept. Fathers can love, but how he shows that love can be different, but that doesn't mean it is not there. Give this heartbreak to God if you have it, and allow him to help you heal.

About Jacob/Israel

Jacob was a trickster and king at lying to get what he wanted. He cheated to get the blessing, and the same trick he played was later played on him with Leah. He had four wives and children from all of them to make the twelve sons of Israel. His beloved Rachel gave him Joseph, who may have looked like his beauty departed. He was heartbroken and trying to move on, but he did show more attention to Joseph, and an example is the coat of many colors he made for him. This caused jealousy and division amongst the brothers that led to faking Joseph's death for his desperate brothers to avenge their jealousy and desire to be seen.

Assignment: If you are grieving the loss of a loved one, or your father is, be patient.

Your Impact: Patient. Some things take time to heal from, and there is no quick solution. We have to show more grace to those stuck in a time and place.

Make it Personal

Reflection

Point 1: Having children with the spouse you love is a powerful feeling.

Point 2: It was the sight he had prayed for, to be with his wife and to have their son grow up with them.

Point 3: When she died giving birth to Benjamin, that caused a void within his heart, possibly, which also made paying more attention to Joseph more desirable.

Point 4: His brothers did not take the time to understand their father, but judged his deeds. They faked the death of Joseph, thinking they could take what was his.

Point 5: Like their uncle Esau, they found they could not take what was not theirs. They could only keep what was theirs, and what they had was more than enough if they only spent time to see what they had.

Affirmation

I will not spend my time growing jealous of what someone else has, nor will I waste my time judging my father for their faults, but instead choose to love them and share mercy to forgive.

Chapter 8
Mordecai

Fathering children born of love is desired, but if you are called to father out of purpose, would you do it? Many fathers are called to father children who are not born of their blood but could be distant or close family members. Mordecai was the uncle of Esther. We don't know how her parents died, only that her uncle fathered her in her parents' absence.

To be a father of choice with no legal or parental obligation is commendable. He was willing to share what belonged to his family with Esther. He invested time and resources to prepare her for the journey ahead. It was Mordecai who helped her navigate getting to the throne.

He showed her what was valuable about her and any woman. He told her how her inner beauty was far more beautiful than any jewelry she could add. He told her to listen to wise counsel. When she was offered the vault of jewelry, the advice from a house staffer told her to keep the piece simple, and she did.

He showed her how to regard a husband and show respect. She submitted to her father, Mordecai, and valued his words. When he told her less is best, she won the King's attention and ultimately his affection. He chose her to be Queen because she was authentic and had the presence of royalty. It takes a father or a father figure to bring this out of a woman.

When she became Queen, he told her how she had a big assignment, even a political calling. Her uncle understood the importance of being queen, and he was clear on how to navigate the legal landscape with a watchful eye. Haman, another subject of the king, saw how Mordecai was advancing in rank, and he thought to stop him. He planned to discredit him, but that backfired. He had integrity and was wise as a serpent but harmless as a dove (Matthew 10:16). He saved the king's life, and it was Haman who had to reward him.

When Haman introduced a bill to kill all the Hebrews, it triggered Mordecai to be strategic in how Esther revealed her identity to the king. He didn't know she was a Hebrew, and that this bill he signed would impact her, too. She had to go before the king to plead her position; the only problem was that she could not come to him unless he called for her. To go before the king unsummoned put you at risk of death.

Esther was scared, but Mordecai warned her that walking away was not an option. She thought, I am sure, she could escape because no one knew that she was Hebrew. Her uncle showed her that seeing her people suffer an injustice was going to be an injustice against her, too. She had to face the giant and speak up for the Kingdom of the Hebrews. She could not run and hide, but had to stand up and fight her battle.

A good father will encourage you to do something you are nervous to do but must do. They will not give you a way of escape, but help prepare you for the journey ahead. He put faith and encouragement behind her and did what she asked when she said to have the whole nation fast.

He helped to build her voice as a queen, and as a father, you will help your sons and daughters develop their voices to speak. Likewise, you will help your wife to be a positive reflection of your leadership, equipped to be herself, and an improved version of who she used to be before you.

About Mordecai

Mordecai was Esther's uncle, who was also a guard of the king. He did the right things concerning the king and acted with integrity. He was noticed by the king for exposing a group determined to kill him, and he was rewarded by the man who wanted him dead. He was a key component of Esther becoming queen and knowing how to walk in her role. He helped to direct her path and remind her of who she was when she needed to know it the most.

Assignment: Fathering children whom you choose, or taking the responsibility for family, receive the flowers owed to you.

Your Impact: Gratitude. If the children you care for never tell you thank you or are ungrateful, may this entry be a statement of thanks.

Make it Personal

Reflection

Point 1: Mordecai was a celebratory man known for his good works in the kingdom.

Point 2: He took on the assignment to raise his niece.

Point 3: He prepared her for the throne and advised her on what to do to make the biggest impression on the king.

Point 4: When she was selected to be Queen, and a law was signed to kill the Hebrews, he encouraged her to stand up for her people.

Point 5: He was a father who encouraged and shared the best parts of himself with his niece.

Affirmation

I will be a beacon of direction for those seeking fatherly advice and remind the people of God where their true beauty stems from, within.

Chapter 9
King Ahab

We sometimes don't have powerful figures in our lives to show us the righteous path. We could be born to families who sin and plan to keep on sinning. Ahab was a king who was described as the worst king, more wicked than all who came before him (1 Kings 16:30). He was a Hebrew king who married a Phoenician princess who worshiped Baal.

He was a king who was not known for his voice but for the voice of his wife. Esther knew how to speak and navigate the relationship she had with the king. She knew that she was not over his authority, but meant to be a support. Jezebel was not of that same mindset. She ruled behind Ahab, and she would take part in the moral decline of the nation of Israel or the Hebrews that Ahab led.

As a Father, Ahab was not a man of his own convictions. He married a woman who got him to worship other gods and even submitted his authority to her direction. She was ruling the kingdom behind his voice. When he went to buy a field from a fellow Hebrew and was told no because he didn't want to sell, he told his wife. She then plotted to kill that man and take what he would not sell (1 Kings 21:1-25).

Jezebel raised up hundreds of false prophets in the city, and Elijah, a mighty man of God, challenged them to prove their gods had no power. None of this convicted them or charged them to change their minds in how they were leading the nation. King Ahab ruled, but also fathered a nation. He was teaching his son how to be just like him, or worse.

His son was raised to be like his parents, lawless and an idol worshiper. He was not rooted in the truths of Yah, nor did he have a heart to serve Him. Their son died after being king for a short two-year period. King Ahab reminds me of young men, especially those who are raised by rappers and other influencers. A fathering spirit doesn't have to be used only by your natural father, but can also be used by others you allow to father you.

Many young people today are allowing people who worship devils to lead them. These men are teaching them a moral code that will send them to hell or damage their heart and soul by seeking money and sex for fulfillment. Baal worship is a desire to indulge in drugs, sex, and all kinds of acts to get money. It is a religion that worships money and sex.

For fathers encouraging their sons to love money or to prize having sex without the required love of God, you are bringing damnation on yourself. You are cursing your seed to bear a penalty that might mean they die young. To be king for only two years is sad. He died young, and many youth today are dying young because their fathers are poor examples.

I heard that a celebrity thanked another celebrity for fathering them as they came into the rap game. The one who fathered him turned out to be a molester, a beater, and a man who slapped his own momma to the floor. He was a nuisance to every artist, a thief, a homosexual who abused men, women, and children. He was not a good example fit to lead or father anyone, but when we don't have a good example of what a father is, we will value the things we can see to justify their words.

But if you were to watch their actions, you would soon see that what they create is dead. What they try to do brings death, disease, jail, or some other unfruitful or deadly outcome. You will see that drinking, drugs, sex, and other acts bring disease, heartbreak, torment, soul-ties, and night terrors. You will see that dancing with the devil may be a pretty sight during the light, but in the dark, it is filled with shifting shadows and unease.

King Ahab raised a son who followed in his footsteps, who should not have. As fathers, it is the goal to raise children to know the way–children that are yours and those who need the fathering gift in you. You may have to be like Mordecai or Paul and raise children who are not yours to see the goodness of Yah and what a good father brings to the world. Affirmation: Father, reverse what I have been taught about women or life not like You, and equip me to follow in Your likeness and not like the world.

About King Ahab

Ahab was a man who had a wife who pulled him away from serving God. She was an aggressive female who was hellbent on bringing down the kingdom of Israel through idol worship. She worked through King Ahab to get what she wanted from anybody, and Ahab taught his son to be and act the same way as him. He was a disappointment to Yah and was said to be the wickedest king to sit on the throne.

Assignment: If you were raised or are being raised by father figures who are not creating the traits you desire as a father, select new father figures who do.

Your Impact: Change. If what you are doing is not working, change. Stop the music, cut out the conversation, switch up your friends, or whatever you need to do to realign your life with virtue.

Make it Personal

Reflection

Point 1: King Ahab was a king who did not rule his kingdom under the principles of God.

Point 2: He married a woman who pulled him away from the principles of Yahweh and taught the people of God to worship Baal instead.

Point 3: His son was also trained up in his way, and that led to a short kingdom reign of just two years.

Point 4: When we don't follow after a father figure set on building us up, we partner with those tearing us down.

Point 5: The cycle of bad and poor fathering can be broken, but it takes getting back to the foundations of God to make any lasting impact.

Affirmation

Father, reverse what I have been taught about women or life not like You, and equip me to follow in Your likeness and not like the world.

Chapter 10
Paul

For men who have been married and are called away from the life they used to live to follow God, it could be a lonely road. It could mean leaving a father, mother, wife, job, city, or country. The Father is so full of grace that He can reach out to those whom the world would say don't deserve His goodness or patience. Paul was a soldier in the army who led the charge to judge Christ followers. He witnessed the deaths of many faithful Christians, like Stephen.

He saw many believers stoned and even participated in taking the lives of believers, later called Christians. He was visited by Yashua, Jesus himself, and asked, "Saul, Saul, why are you persecuting Me?" Paul was doing what he thought was right, but it wasn't right; he later found out. Sometimes we can live a life that doesn't line up with our purpose, but our gifts are given without repentance (Romans 11:29).

Paul was a convert of the church after the vision on

the Damascus Road, where he was struck blind and sent to learn the truth of Jesus for three years (Acts 9). He took the time to learn about whose people he was killing. Have you become a hater of those who love God, or Jesus the Christ, thinking by persecuting, denying, or laughing at those who believe you are doing God a favor?

If the Father sent His Son to come to you and ask, "(Your Name) why are you persecuting Me?" We can blame it on not knowing, we can say it was the church, or our parents. I would encourage you to take the time to learn who Christ is and then decide if your actions are wise or not. The Father is not afraid to reason with you (Isaiah 1:18). What I love that anyone can see about the life of Paul is that for those who have been forgiven much, they love much (Luke 7:47).

Paul wrote most of the New Testament, and the same Christians he was responsible for killing, he was now gifted to speak life to many sons and daughters of Yah. He was called to travel to nations and plead the case of Christ. He was shipwrecked many times, put in jail, and came close to death. He once got bitten by a cobra and didn't flinch because he knew his time was not yet.

He had a thorn in his side because the Father wanted to keep him humble, because he wielded so much power. Many learned to call on him for guidance, fathering in the spiritual sense. He was a father figure to Timothy, a man born of a Hebrew mother and Greek father. He was raised by his mother and grandmother. He had no father figure in his home.

His father, from what we can understand, was gone, and it was Paul who stepped in like a father to guide him.

Many men out here today need a father to step in and help guide them. A man who is not trying to sleep with their mother or take something from them, but is willing to give with clean hands. Paul didn't try to seduce his mother or grandmother, but poured into him to help guide him in the things of God.

I commend all fathers who are willing to use their time to father children not their own, and who stand to receive no direct benefit from giving. It is with this heart that the fathering spirit can be released within the body of Christ to save souls who are fatherless. In many churches, seeing a male youth leader has an incredible influence. Young people need to see spiritually endowed men who can father them to do the right thing.

Women can speak, but fathers train and help to build confidence and conviction. Even with single mothers, they do need an example to help raise the children in their households and community. If a church is ever wondering what ministry they can do to help their community, pouring into the youth will never be a depleted need.

This need is growing. With too many youth being raised by technology and believing sayings that will lead them to a life separate from God, we must take the time to speak into their lives and show them how to love God and see themselves how He does. I challenge you to find at least one young man to pour into. To buy lunch on a regular basis and check up on him.

You will find that children who have a positive male, fathering presence do better in life. It is no secret that there is a benefit to having an active father in the household. If you can be that for someone–you don't have to be a father to learn how to walk with a fathering spirit, but you must have a desire to father. Becoming a father is a process, and you won't get it all right, but you can build a connection and work to become a good father.

Paul had children of his own and a family before his ministry. There isn't much in the Bible to tell us what happened within his own family. What we do know, however, is that he was a great father figure to many. He would call himself the least of the apostles, but we might argue differently. He was a man, previously named Saul before his conversion, when he became Paul, the father of many new believers.

About Paul

Paul was once a married man with children. It is not discussed in the Bible what came about for his family, but his commitment to raise up believers in the knowledge of God is self-evident. He was a mentor and father figure to saints like Timothy. He was a man of standards, and he walked in power. He became the apostle who wrote a lot of the New Testament, but the thorn in his side kept him humble. He always maintained a willingness to be a father and did not require love or affection from mothers to do so.

Assignment: The church and single mothers need men who are willing to help them and not abuse their trust to help them with their children.

Your Impact: Selfless. There is a demand for men who can help women without a hidden agenda for a relationship or sex as a trade for their influence and help.

Make it Personal

Reflection

Point 1: Paul was a man who remained celibate and single during the time of his ministry.

Point 2: He was a man who learned Christ and was faithful to serve Him after the day of his conversion.

Point 3: He wrote most of the New Testament and was used mightily to evangelize to the lost from all nations.

Point 4: He was a father figure to Timothy, a young man born of a Hebrew mother and Greek father.

Point 5: He poured into children with no expectation of a romantic relationship with anyone, but with a heart to bless the Kingdom of God.

Affirmation

I will be honorable in my attempt to father other children who are not born of my household

Chapter 11
King Saul

Before a boy becomes a man, isn't it amazing how much some of them change? For the better, or for the worse, people can change their response to life and challenges. King Saul, before becoming king, was a man from the small tribe of Benjamin. He was an underdog if there ever was one.

He didn't come from a wealthy family, he wasn't the oldest, and he didn't have a whole lot of confidence. When he was selected to be king, he was shocked and thought that Samuel should pick someone else (1 Samuel 9:21). Has your name ever been called at a time when you thought surely there must be a mistake? This was how King Saul felt. He was a man who was faithful to his father and could follow directions.

When his father lost donkeys on his farm, Saul went to seek them out. It was said that King Saul learned the voice of God. He knew Yah in a personal way, and he needed this connection to be the first king. He was tall, dark-haired, and looked like a king, although he did not have the confidence or reputation.

His reputation and confidence were built by God within him. He was following God's commands and having great success. He was given praise by his people, and it would appear that his social rating was high. As long as he followed Yah's commands, he would fight and win battles. Everyone loved him, and he loved being loved.

I would say that King Saul's weakness came back out again when he achieved success. If we don't keep our eyes on Yah, we can become a version of our former selves. He was not confident when he was first picked, and it did his heart good to be selected. At first, he realized that it was God who picked him. Unfortunately, later, he acted as if it were the people who had picked him.

He sought to please people and disobeyed God's command. He was judged for his actions, and those actions would mean his offspring would not inherit the throne but King David instead. King Saul battled with accepting this prophecy, but he knew he couldn't change it. He heard the songs in the streets say that King Saul has slain thousands but King David has slain tens of thousands and he was pissed (1 Samuel 18:6-9).

He wanted to be the prize for the nation and ensure the throne for his son, Jonathan, who was good friends with David. When David was young, he slew Goliath because King Saul was too scared to fight him. King David not only fought the Philistines for disrespecting Yah, but he also won!

He was giving a daughter of Saul to marry because

he won that incredible battle. So now, the daughter and the son of King Saul loved King David. Jonathan already released the throne to him and acknowledged that God chose David and not him to be the next king. King Saul hated that his son gave up what he thought he had worked for.

He was so pissed at Johnathan he threw a javelin at him seeking to injure or even kill him. King Saul had a violent streak, but the streak was fueled by jealousy, envy, and anger. He didn't dare use that same power to kill a Philistine. He stayed locked away, but one day he would die on the battle ground same as his son, Jonathan.

When Jonathan died, King David cried for him because they were good friends. Jonathan once saved David's life and also did other favors for him. Saul hated that his son loved David and was his friend. This hatred leaked into his fathering and meant he could not be a good father because he allowed him being disgruntled for losing the throne to cloud his affection and direction.

He never blamed himself for losing the throne, but others, and he even blamed his son and tried to take that anger out on him. Pray for the fathers who blame others for their shortcomings. Who still battle to accept their faults and how their choices cost them loss. As children of fathers who struggled in this area, it is paramount that you forgive so you don't become a product of that anger.

The same vice that fuels their anger desires to fuel yours; don't allow it, but instead fight to remain blameless and pray for those who despitefully use you (Philippians 2:15, Matthew 5:44-45). Fathers may use your kindness and assume you are ignorant or weak, but the Father who sits in heaven has the last say.

About King Saul

King Saul was a humble man entrusted to care for donkeys and farm animals. He was selected from a meek tribe of Benjamin, and he was anointed to be king by Samuel. He became a people pleaser, and that meant he disobeyed God. He grew furious with his son and resorted to physical violence to express his disapproval. He could not father his son as he should have because he was consumed by the consequences of his own actions that he took out on Jonathan and anyone in close proximity.

Assignment: For those living with abusive fathers, and the many who blame others for their own faults, do not take their blame into your heart.

Your Impact: Accountability. Every man must be responsible for their own choices. Their choices are not yours, although we have to deal with them, we can choose not to own them.

Make it Personal

Reflection

Point 1: Started with humble beginnings and the ability to follow directions.

Point 2: He was chosen as the first king of the Hebrews because the people asked Yah for one.

Point 3: He started to believe that his accomplishments were his and not God's, so he attempted to please people and not God.

Point 4: He was violent to his son and also to David. He threw objects at him and attempted to kill both of them several times.

Point 5: His uncontrollable rage stemmed from his own disobedience. He could not accept accountability for his mistakes but tried to blame everyone else.

Affirmation

Today, I take accountability for my mistakes and I ask that God, You help me to right wrongs I can and to do better than I have.

Chapter 13
Abraham

It is not easy to be present in two households. It can be tempting to stay in a relationship to keep your family together, but sometimes divorce or breakups are necessary. Abraham was between a rock and a hard place, and he could not keep his family together. The father of Isaac, but also Ishmael, was a good father who showed up for both of his sons, who lived in different homes and were worlds apart.

Being a good father to children you don't live with is a huge undertaking we cannot take lightly. It is not easy to be there to call, stop by, or spend time when women can make this hard or impossible. Abraham was born to a father who didn't raise him. Terah was a man who worshiped many gods and even made figurings, idols for the King Nimrod. He feared for the life of his son and even lied and killed another baby in his place to spare his life.

The ability to lie to avoid trouble, Abraham learned from his father. When he pushed over his father's idols in his house, he left shortly after. He didn't stick around to find out what came next, but ran. When he ran, he fled to the house of a relative who raised him.

In the Apocrypha book, Jasher, we learn that Abraham was raised by a relative, Shem, Noah's son (Jasher 9:5). Shem knew the Word of God and his culture very well. He was not caught up in the plans of Nimrod or practicing idol worship. He instilled fundamental truths into Abraham about Yah. Although Shem was like a second father to Abraham, his birth father's influence and character were still pumping in his veins.

Abraham was a God fearing man, but he was fearful. He was afraid when he went into Egypt with his wife to claim her. He told her to lie and say they were siblings. God had to interfere to keep her virtue. He didn't do this once but twice. He didn't care about the plagues or problems that would befall others because he lied. The Egyptian King even asked in Genesis 20, "What hast thou done unto us? and what have I offended thee, that thou hast brought on me and on my kingdom a great sin? thou hast done deeds unto me that ought not to be done...11 And Abraham said, Because I thought, Surely the fear of God is not in this place; and they will slay me for my wife's sake."

He was a flawed man and perhaps a terrible husband at times. But! He knew how to please Yah with his faith and loyalty. Fathers are not perfect, but can still be good fathers. Fathering Ishmael with Hagar, he did at the behest of his wife, Sarah. She, too, would sacrifice his choice to please her ideas and maintain her image. She wanted a son, and he gave her a son.

However, she had been promised to bear a son herself, but she was impatient to wait on Yah. Abraham heard the prophecy and believed, but Sarah laughed in her heart, and the Father asked why she laughed (Genesis 18:12-15). Ishmael came into the world through people's decisions, but the Father still chose to bless him. He wasn't Yah's plan, but a plan of man that he made work to their favor.

When he was born, Sarah loved him, and so did Abraham. It wasn't a problem so much with the young man; Sarah had the issue with Hagar. Hagar became prideful and thought she was more valuable than Sarah because she bore Abraham a son. But like how an elephant's baby can take two years to be born because of the size and purpose, Sarah had to wait on her child with a big destiny.

As the young man grew and his baby brother came along, it was tension between the women, and that tension spread to the children. However, it could be concluded that Sarah wanted to avoid any misunderstanding of what Isaac stood to inherit. It was out of that mind that she demanded that Ishmael, her chosen mistake, be removed to protect Isaac's inheritance (Genesis 21:16).

Abraham had to do what was best for the wife he committed to, and he sent his son and Hagar away. Although he sent Hagar away, he never thought of abandoning his son. His son was much older than what we think from the Bible stories we watched on tv. He wasn't a baby but a man who could be considered a young adult.

When he left, God provided, and Abraham knew that He would. He gave both of his sons to Yah to lead and guide, and he trusted those plans. In the Apocrypha book Jasher, you will find that Abraham would go and visit Ishmael when he started his family. He went by his home, and he was out, so he left an encrypted message for him that he understood to mean that his wife was terrible, so get another one (Jasher 25:17).

Ishmael got the message, and that wife he put away and selected another. The second wife, when Abraham met her, she greeted him and was kind, and he left another encrypted message to say she was a good wife. He kept that wife. He wouldn't know the code if he didn't know his father's voice and teachings.

Abraham kept seeing his son without being wrapped up with Hagar, or his baby momma. It is possible to keep a bond with your child even if you do not fully engage in communication or actions with your child's mother anymore. There should be a safe distance between the two of you to avoid any relapse or bits of confusion.

Something you would also find out about Abraham was that he made sure his sons knew each other. When Abraham was asked by Yah to sacrifice Isaac, he was a grown man. He wasn't a teenager, again like in the movies, but an adult. On this journey to the mountain where he was to be sacrificed, Ishmael also came. He journeyed as far as Yah would allow him to go before Abraham had to stop him and ask him to wait for them to return, and he did (Jasher Chapter 23).

Abraham and Isaac learned to get along and build a bond that their children may know nothing about. Their relationship and beef were set aside during the life of Abraham, and it would be his will for it to remain that way. Although Ishmael is the oldest, he is not the rightful heir to the throne of Abraham. He was not the son of promise, but God made a way to include him in His plan of mercy and grace.

Yah can do the same for you by including children you had before your marriage to be part of your story and bless God. There can be children who were born of promise and those who came about because we made choices that brought them here. God can make both cases work for your good and show mercy like he did with Abraham and Judah (Genesis 38:20–26).

About Abraham

Abraham was the father of many nations and received the promise of God to be His people. He was a man who was raised to do right, although he carried fear in his heart. He lied many times to avoid problems, but he was a man who would give anything to God, the Father. He gave both his sons into Yah's hands, and he blessed both nations. He kept a relationship with them both and respected his wife in the process.

Assignment: Being a good father doesn't mean you have no flaws. You can have fear, or make mistakes, but allow the Father to redeem you.

Your Impact: Balance. It takes balance to be active for multiple children or in multiple houses. You don't have to give up on your children because women are a problem. Pray for a bridge and connection with your children and amongst your children.

Make it Personal

Reflection

Point 1: Abraham was born to a father who was an idol worshipper.

Point 2: He was raised by a family member who taught him in the ways of God.

Point 3: He was willing to lie to avoid trouble because, although he was full of faith, he was also fearful.

Point 4: He maintained a relationship with both his sons from both houses without crossing the line with his wife, Sarah.

Point 5: There was nothing Abraham would not give to Yah, and that made him faithful in the sight of God, and He blessed him immensely.

Affirmation

I will be a father who will balance my life and not allow the issues between the mothers of my children to bring division between me and my children.

Chapter 12
King David

We don't have to be perfect to be used by Yah, but we want to have a heart for God. Having a heart for God can help you endure and power through life's challenges that will come. A man after God's own heart was David. He was a man who knew God and allowed Him to shepherd him.

King David was the type of man who worshiped God so hard through dance that his clothes shook to the ground. He was not a coward and never ran from a fight that he was meant to stand and fight. He was a mighty warrior full of wisdom, faith, and strategy.

David secured friendships and marriages that furthered his influence on the nation of Israel. Jonathan, his best friend, loved him and helped him win battles that his father had hoped to win. He could play the harp so well that King Saul would call him in to play and send his demons away. He needed David to soothe his worries and fears through playing an instrument. His anointing was moving, and it was powerful.

He had a humble story, also. He was the youngest of a large family, and he spent most of his time caring for sheep. He would fight off lions, bears, and other wild animals to keep them from harming the sheep. He was faithful in caring for the animals, and he did his job with exceptional execution. He impressed Yah, and He chose to acknowledge him before men.

Defeating Goliath was a major milestone to put his name in the mouths of his people. Although he was put into a song that praised his greatness, he also had a dark side to his life. David loved women. He had several wives but hundreds of concubines. Who's to say how many children he honestly had with so many women in his life, and to describe what kind of relationship he had with them would also leave more blank pages.

What we can speak about are the children raised by his wives. He had three sons and a daughter, who are spoken about in the Bible specifically. One of his sons raped his daughter Tamar. When this happened, he did not discipline this son at all. I often thought, maybe he didn't discipline his son because he, too, was guilty of the same thing.

In the Bible, it talks about how he took Bathsheba and brought her to him, and he lay with her. He knew she was committed and married, but he didn't care about that. It could be concluded that he kidnapped and raped Bathsheba (2 Samuel 11-12:25). If so, is it a wonder why he had such a low respect for the value of women, even for his own daughter?

Absalom felt his response was poor, and so he

sought to avenge his sister. He killed his brother, and David was sad about that. He mourned more for the outcome of his lack of discipline than for the incident that caused the issue. He didn't father his children or create a strong foundation for them. Even when Absalom sought to take the kingdom from him, he was the son born to King Saul's daughter, David's first wife; he didn't do anything.

He could not bring himself to defend himself against his son, who wanted to kill him. It was his guard who defended him and ultimately killed his son. It broke his heart to see his sons die in this manner. King Solomon was the only one of the three who became king, and he was a wise man. I am not sure if this gift came from his father, mother, or was a unique answered prayer for Solomon to be wise, but he got the gift. King Solomon was a product of his father, because he had even more concubines than David.

He had over a thousand, and his father had hundreds. The difference was that Solomon was taking away from God and started to worship other gods over Yahweh. It is painful to see how our negative attributes can rub off on our children. If we could pick, we would pick the best parts of ourselves and leave the ugly things behind. Life, unfortunately, doesn't work like this.

It is important to make time for our children and even take a break from love and sex to assist them and spend time with them. It could be said that David had no time for his children because he was too busy chasing women in his downtime. He was walking the rooftop and saw Bathsheba bathing. What was he doing up there like an eagle stalking prey? He could have been playing a game with his sons or spending time doing anything else.

As men and Fathers, we must set aside time to build a loving relationship with our spouse, yes, but also to raise our children. Children need our time and attention. We cannot be so busy providing for them and doing the things we think need to be done to provide, that we forget to spend time with them. King David was a good king, but he was hardly there for his children.

If you are guilty of working too much and not being present to build a relationship with your children, consider changing your routine. Create events to support quality time as often as you can. Go to parks, play games, pray, and just spend time. Sharing love doesn't have to be complicated, but it can speak volumes and protect sensitive hearts.

About King David

King David was a man who was great at many things. He was gifted in the arts, a great defender, and a lover of God. He struggled romantically and was one of the biggest whoremongers in the Bible only second to his son, King Solomon. He was busy fighting wars through his reign, and when he had downtime, it could be understood that he spent that time with other women. As a man, it is important to balance the love you have for God, women, and, I dare say a woman, and spending time with your children. All three need your love and affection.

Assignment: Women are a blessing to human creation. They were designed to be a helpmeet, and they deserve your time, but not all of it.

Your Impact: Self-Worth. If you want to build a legacy, you need to build a connection. You cannot have a serious connection with one-night stands. Women who rob you of a divine connection with your children and God are not a blessing but a slow death to your future.

Make it Personal

Reflection

Point 1: King David had a humble beginning, but he found ways to please God and be named a man after God's own heart.

Point 2: He had hundreds of concubines, won many wars, and was a gifted artist.

Point 3: He was on a mission to bring the Kingdom of Israel together.

Point 4: He did not discipline his children and likely didn't know all of his children.

Point 5: Even though he fell short of his assignment to father the children he bore, God made him a promise to always have a descendant of King David on the throne.

Affirmation

I don't have to be perfect for God to use my life, but I will use the rest of my life to give Him glory.

Chapter 14
The Close

Fathering is a needed role in any society. If we are talking about the natural or supernatural realm, we all need a father. Boys and girls, men and women, we need a father to help guide our path. If you have not had a good relationship or a relationship at all with your father, I pray you have found something you needed to hear in the pages of this book.

This book is not an exhaustive checklist for what makes a good father, but highlights key elements from fathers' lives in the bible and shows how those lives can help to pull a father's life back into focus. If you are not a father yet, or your children have passed on, this book is written to activate your fathering gift.

You are needed in this world today to help speak life into the lives of young people being raised by poor role models. People who are more like King Ahab and are not sending them in the right direction. People who idolize sex, or the perversion of it, the love of money, and what all they will do to have it. We have to break this daydream over society and those called by the name of the Lord.

If you are looking for a way to become a better father today, bring discipline out of love to your home. To establish a standard for your children to follow, which you also try to implement. No, you won't be perfect, and neither will they. Some of your children will have children out of wedlock. Some will go to jail, some will lie, cheat, or steal.

As a father, you will help to hold them accountable so they learn. You will encourage single mothers to hold their children accountable and allow them to grow up. They cannot be babies forever, and no parent should allow guilt to rob them of parenting. Be like Yahweh and set the foundation for their life. Be like the Prodigal Son's Father and welcome them home when they want to do right, but let them know the rules.

If they choose to stay, they are going to have to submit to your authority. As children learn to submit to authority, you don't have to worry about them in the streets or about them failing at relationships. Yes, you can teach your children how to do everything right, but they can still meet death, heartbreak, or an unfavorable outcome. This is not a judgment against your fathering or a punishment for your past life.

Like Job, sometimes the father brags on you, and the enemy gets to test your faith. Don't cave, but also be open to grieve. Jacob might have struggled with the death of his wife, but his sons came around to see that he needed Joseph in his life to survive. Although it was painful for them to feel ignored, it was heartwrenching to see him fade away without him.

Sometimes we have to decrease so that the Father can increase in those we love. When our children need us, or even if they think they do not, give them structure, the truth, and love. You can love your children and judge the sin, like the Prodigal Son's Father. You do not have to allow your children to come back home with the baby to continue dating, which opens the chance for more problems.

You should cut that off and make them live a life accountable for the child they already have. No, they might not like it, but your house, your rules. The lack of rules is how they ended in the situation; now they can learn from their mistakes. A loving father helps his children to learn from mistakes and not continue in them. So, cutting off lustful connections or relationships that go nowhere is part of being a father.

If your son or daughter is hanging out with the wrong crowd, separate them from that, or make them get out. If your child doesn't want to honor your rules for dating with the intention of marriage after they have built up their own self-worth, they can leave, too. The prodigal son got the boot to do what he wanted out there, and guess what? He returned home humbled with the intention to get right. Some of your children need to come to you and not you running to them. Let them grow up!

You cannot be a father who has no consequences like Eli because you are afraid of their choices or reaction to your requirements. Do the right thing anyway, and the Father will judge you as faithful. You can stop or prevent sins from happening in your home.

Lastly, if your father has caused you pain, discomfort, or has been absent from your life. We have to allow God to heal our hearts and mend the mistakes others make. It doesn't mean He washes them away, but He can take away the pain and bring forgiveness. He can take away judgment and help usher in understanding.

If you feel like you are in bondage with an addiction, chasing women, working too much, or not finding balance, there is a Savior who can redeem your time! He can make every crooked path straight in your life and help restore the life you thought was over. He gave Job back his life and gave him double for his trouble. He gave Paul a new mission after he had killed many Christians.

He can give you a new life too and help you to start over–even with your flaws. He can use you to be a father and bring out the best in you for others to learn from.

Blessings, Shalom.

Prayer

May we end this book in Prayer.

Father, we thank You for being here with us and reminding us of the importance of fatherhood. Father's Day is a day when many feel alone, abandoned, or struggle with mixed emotions. May You clean our hearts and renew our sense of expectation.

May You heal the fathers in our community so that they can be fathers that our communities need. May You lift them up and protect them so that they can protect their families. May You equip them with wisdom, knowledge, resources, and support to father.

May You take everything meant to be for their bad and turn it for their good! May You bring forgiveness where it is needed. May You provide them with helpmeets that don't mind working with them and helping to support the vision he has that supports their own. May they have partners, associates, administrators, and other helps to support the vision for how You want them to move in this season.

Prayer

Thank You that You did not create men to have to live life alone. May You bring balance and show them like You did Isaac, who their wives should be. May You make it plain. May You help them with balance and focus. Help them to discern the spirits of women who mean them well and those who are sent on assignment to tear down.

Father, we need fathers who have a heart to father with Your love, patience, understanding, mercy, and grace. May they extend grace to their family members and be not easily offended. May You help to establish emotional stability and maturity so that they can be a strong tower in the times of need for their families. May You give them families who can support them through hard times and pray them through trouble.

May You help them know they are not alone, but You are here warring for them. You are here to keep them going when they want to quit. For those battling damaging thoughts, may they see them being here is part of the plan. Though the enemy comes in like a flood, You will raise a standard in them. You will help them come out on top, although the enemy surrounds them. Though they walk through the valley of dry bones, You will give them favor.

Prayer

May You anoint their heads, their business, their future, their dreams, and provide them with confidence to shake the nations. May they be bold as a lion, sent on assignment to build the Kingdom of God by the Power of God. Fill them with Your Spirit and show them the way to please You. Keep them safe through their journey and watch over their families. Block the enemy from being successful with divorce, teenage pregnancy, dropping out of school, drugs, addiction, lying, poverty, mental anguish, confusion, self-doubt, and the spirit of rebellion.

We come against every Jezebel and the spirit of Ahab in their lives. May they fight to be holy, and if they should fail, for them to come to You because You care for them. May You make their burdens light and their yoke easy. May their latter days be better than the former days. Restore their homes, minds, peace, wealth, and future. May You reset their sexual appetites and shift their focus to the things that are higher, for Your thoughts are not ours.

Prayer

Bless them and the works of their hands. Bless their spouses and their children. Keep their mind and their strength.

In the Mighty Name of Yashua, Hallelujah and So Be It!

May you be renewed and refreshed today.

Shalom

Chapter About the Author

"God blesses those who work for peace, for they will be called the children of God." Matthew 5:9

Krystal Lee is proud to have authored this book and accompanying course to better readers' lives. She has a heart for helping people in their deepest times of need. She writes because she believes there is power in sharing stories and life accounts that others can benefit from and learn from. Sharing is caring, so she shares stories, ideas, and resources to better the lives of her readers.

In addition, Dr. Lee has authored over 35 books across twelve or more genres (adult, children, youth fiction, self-help, spiritual growth, novels, and more), in addition to ghostwriting and editing more than 20 published works. She has launched coaching programs and web courses that helped formulate many startup companies. Her specialty is aiding coaches, creatives, and service-based companies in defining their message, brand, unique selling point, and client avatar, as well as generating a sales cycle and structure for her clients.

Website
AuthorKLee.com

Empowering individuals is at the core of her work, and she is driven by her passion to continue writing. In addition to being an author, Krystal Lee is a business owner of multiple companies, a consultant, an ordained chaplain, and a speaker.

For more information about Dr. Krystal Lee, scan the QR. To engage with the Coaching series and Monthly Meet up Group for Embrace Your Crown First Sundays at 4pm, please use the QR or visit InviteEyc.com and EmbraceYourCrown.com

Website
EmbraceYourCrown.com

AuthorKLee.com Creator of *WAE Process*

Explore over seven different book genres, and find something suitable for every member of the family.

www.ingramcontent.com/pod-product-compliance
Lightning Source LLC
Chambersburg PA
CBHW060252030426
42335CB00014B/1661